RISING HIGHER

RISING HIGHER

ROWAN EVERHART

CONTENTS

CHAPTER 1

Introduction to Personal and Professional Developm

My career has always focused on leadership development, but the longer I've worked, the more I've come to understand the critical connection between leading myself and leading others. The journey toward effective leadership begins with personal leadership. Throughout this book, I'll refer to these as simply Developing Questions. These questions are essential for those who lead smaller teams, and they're designed to prompt reflection on yourself, your team, and your work. Each question follows the "I ask it because I'll make a difference" format.

In addition to the questions, this book provides supporting reference articles that can be used by individuals or small groups working with a facilitator. These references are meant to provoke thought and discussion about the Twelve Questions, which are crucial for personal and professional development.

Furthermore, this book includes numerous examples, stories, action reminders, and personal practices. Business schools can't always prepare people for leadership because leadership is a unique experience that often requires a personal touch. Many of us take an informal path to leadership by leading ourselves. We learn by becoming more self-aware, setting goals, and developing strategies to navigate the choices we face. Sometimes, though, we need guidance—or even a push. **That's where "Rising Higher" comes in, offering you the necessary guidance and incentive.**

Lee Colan starts with basic questions about leadership, emphasizing that leadership always begins with leading ourselves and then extends to include others in organizations, companies, communities, friendships, and families. **We are all leaders, but we also rely on the leadership of others.** Leaders often turn to seminars, workshops, or books to learn new things, challenge themselves, or get motivated. The most successful leaders never lose their eagerness to learn; they continually seek new methods, ideas, and cutting-edge thinking.

Personal Management is akin to Relationship Management and Change Management. These three sets of skills address how we lead—ourselves, our relationships, and our organizations. It's important to always consider the balance needed when addressing the Development Questions. Leadership is not just an abstract concept; it is a practical and concrete art. With "Rising Higher," Lee Colan's questions provide robust support for an inspiring and thought-provoking journey toward personal development. As you travel this road, let the Twelve Questions guide you.

Understanding the Significance of Personal Growth

Why should you develop a greater understanding of yourself? There are countless right answers to this question. In our complex and advanced world, understanding oneself is crucial to navigating the opportunities and challenges we encounter. Understanding oneself is the foundation of all achievements and failures. To grow into effective leaders, we must first manage our personal growth, which forms the basis of leadership development. Thus, understanding oneself is paramount for both leadership and personal development in any domain.

This understanding helps us recognize our strengths and weaknesses. Only by understanding these can we develop the maturity needed to lead ourselves and others. The concept of self-understanding is of extraordinary importance, which is why this book poses several questions early on, focusing on you. I am confident you will find great value in these questions. Take the time to reflect deeply and honestly. Be true to yourself, bury your ego, and demonstrate humility, at least while reading these sections.

Policymakers must also understand themselves. Knowing their strengths and limitations allows them to rely on personal intuition and judgment effectively. This self-awareness empowers them to make better decisions and lead more effectively.

Question 1: What Are My Core Values?

The first essential question often gets passed over, and that, in my opinion, is to our great peril. What is each of our unique sets of core values? Values are like a guiding light along our journey of life; they help us to make the right decisions. Without them, we are left to drift, to shrug our shoulders when choices are presented, and then to wonder, "why me?" when really uninspiring things start to happen. The problem is, when we have not consciously considered what each of our unique sets of personal core values are, it is as though an internal moral compass is amiss. If it is lost altogether, we lie in danger of self-selection or, worse still, manipulation into roles, environments, and situations that are not truly us, and which often go completely against our true nature.

In reality, our values should inform, affect, and predict our behaviors, judgments, and morals. Whether it is our own personal yardstick, the "helping hand" of those we care for and love, or the beacon for those we lead. In order to determine what your core values are, both individually and collectively, you must first start by understanding what they actually represent.

We all possess "individual-organizational," "individual-familial," "individual-professional," and "individual-relationship" sets of core values, so in the first instance, it is best to identify which set you are searching for. This is crucial, as it ensures that conflicts between personal and professional values are kept to a minimum. Each set carries its own unique features, each set acts independently, and each set evolves and changes independently too.

Defining Core Values

At first sight, defining core values may seem like an easy exercise. You are asked to think of the five most important attributes that guide your behavior every day. While this seems straightforward, it can be quite challenging, as values are the foundation of judgment and decision-making. In fact, every single person I have ever met in my life believed they were excellent decision-makers. Yet, it's the clarity and prioritization of core values that truly underpin sound decision-making.

Important decisions are rooted in our core values. A decision-maker does not treat values like items stored in life's closet, to be taken out only when the situation demands, and then crammed back in afterward. Instead, a decision-maker places their three to five most important values prominently on display every single day, applying them regularly and predictably.

Allow me to give you one small example to illustrate this. If you write down the 15 most important values in your life, you will often see that numbers six through 15 are neglected. In my experiment, values six through 15 were displayed in my office and at home as wall art, constantly referring to them. However, without consistent application, they remain mere decor and do not influence daily decisions.

So ask yourself, are your fifth through 15th most important values aligned in the best manner possible to allow you to reach peak performance at work or in family life? This is not to suggest that you cannot have it all, but rather to highlight the importance of paying more attention to your core set of values in your decision-making processes. For this reason, the journey to personal and professional satisfaction begins by clearly defining our values.

This exercise in defining core values is not only foundational but transformative. It compels us to examine what truly matters, helps us navigate complex choices, and ensures we remain true to our authentic selves. So, take the time to contemplate and define your core values with a deep sense of honesty and commitment.

CHAPTER 3

Question 2: What Are My Strengths and Weaknesses?

Career planning and personal empowerment plans are built on a critical and concomitant pair of questions: "What are my strengths?" and "What are my weaknesses?" A major reason people flounder long and hard before realizing their goals is an inability to answer the most fundamental questions: "Who am I?" We often undervalue our strengths while lacking the courage to face our weaknesses honestly. These judgments reflect a curious lack of enthusiasm for being brave, adventurous, and truly alive.

This same lack of enthusiasm makes me nervous when I hear too much praise for strength finder dimensions, intelligence quotients, personalized learning plans, teamwork inventories, and the favorite motivational techniques of successful executives. Reducing the human spirit to a bunch of numbers may warm the soul of any accountant, but it often fails to capture the essence of our true capabilities. Leadership, at its core, is about more than just scores and assessments. It's about genuine courage and humility, qualities that these tools sometimes overlook.

A second, more worrisome issue is the mistaken emphasis on the cult of personality. In our society, money and status are often seen as the ultimate measures of success. With them, personal strengths and weaknesses become tokens to be massaged and polished in preparation for endless banquets, public appearances, press interviews, and academic chairmanships. Familiar, though ultimately useless, recommendations to stay grounded, maintain close personal relationships, or work closely with advisers perpetuate this myth. There is something fundamentally wrong when the pursuit of a good life is reduced to a search for status and material wealth.

Personality-based models often underemphasize the crucial significance of our environment and its hidden patterns on our collective intelligence and the quality of our lives. We must be more ambitious in understanding how to find and embrace our true selves. In the next insight, we shall learn how to uncover our hidden potential. To truly understand ourselves, we need to become masters of our own dark domains.

Identifying Strengths and Weaknesses

In recent years, the concept of life possibilities developed by Donald O. Clifton, known as the "father" of the positive psychology approach, has gained great relevance. His proposal suggests that people should not focus solely on correcting their weaknesses but also identify their strengths and continue to develop them. This idea has significantly impacted the Human Resources departments of many companies. Currently, the incorporation of diagnostic and operational behavior (dob) software is part of corporate strategic planning. The objective is to offer resources that assess the skills, convictions, talents, and positive attributes of employees and manage these characteristics effectively.

One of the questions nearly everyone faces at some point in their professional career is: Should I correct my deficiencies or not? If a deficiency prevents practical and efficient professional performance, then the answer is yes. However, if it is a minor deficiency overshadowed by a strong, active ability, then the answer is no.

Identifying our strengths and weaknesses requires introspection and a willingness to face uncomfortable truths. It involves acknowledging our limitations while also recognizing and nurturing our inherent talents. The journey to personal and professional satisfaction begins by clearly defining our strengths and weaknesses. This clarity not only helps us navigate our careers more effectively but also empowers us to make more informed and confident decisions.

Understanding our strengths allows us to leverage them to our advantage, maximizing our potential and impact. Meanwhile, acknowledging our weaknesses helps us develop strategies to mitigate them, ensuring they do not hinder our progress. This balanced approach to self-assessment is crucial for continuous growth and development.

In conclusion, the journey to personal and professional empowerment starts with a deep and honest assessment of our strengths and weaknesses. Embrace this process with courage and enthusiasm, and let it guide you toward a more fulfilling and successful life.

CHAPTER 4

Question 3: How Can I Set Effective Goals?

Do you have a goal each day, each year, for your life? Are you reaching your goals? Do you celebrate your achievements? If not, why? As the saying goes, by failing to prepare, you prepare to fail. Your ability to set effective goals reflects your motivation, persistence, and discipline. In life, you have choices: you can complete a task, or you can offer excuses for why you did not. Nearly everyone who is successful at anything gets that way because of goal setting. Goals give you a purpose, a direction, and motivation. They provide a standard to which you can hold yourself accountable. They enable you to live productively and courageously rather than reactively.

Setting effective goals is one of the most important actions a person can take to grow. Well-defined goals can motivate you to take action, overcome procrastination, and make use of time and resources. Describe your long-term visions, turn these into definite short-term objectives, and then create specific, measurable achievements on which task actions are defined. The major attributes of goal setting are to permit people to know what is important, to control their lives, to facilitate determination and commitment, to improve decision-making, to enhance anxiety tolerance, to stimulate peak performance, to lead to periods of self-expansion, and to provide positive attention.

The SMART Goal Setting Framework

Goals differ from wishes, hopes, and desires. A goal contains a strong plan of action and is precisely defined. The SMART Goal setting framework was designed to help you ensure that your goals are structured effectively. SMART is an acronym for five key elements: Specific, Measurable, Achievable, Realistic, and Time-Bound. Let's take a closer look at what each of these elements signifies.

Specific: The more specific a goal, the better, as it leaves no space for ambiguity. The more details a goal contains about what is supposed to be accomplished, the more likely it is that the goal will be achieved. The six "W" questions should be answered while creating a goal: "Who," "What," "When," "Where," "Which," and "Why." For example, a person may set a goal to "do well at work." This goal would be better defined if she said she will do well at work by becoming more proficient in her tasks, communicating with her superior and coworkers more effectively, and engaging in projects with accuracy and initiative.

Measurable: Goals should be quantifiable. If a goal is measurable, it becomes possible to define indicators to measure the degree to which the goal has been attained. Choosing indicators for a goal not only helps to determine what information is needed to assess performance, but it also helps you hold yourself accountable for making progress. For example, although an aspiring model might aim to lose weight, a more measurable goal would be to strive for a body mass index (BMI) below a certain number, calculated using height and weight measurements.

Achievable: An achievable goal is one that is feasible, practical, and attainable. A person should assess whether she has the necessary resources, knowledge, and time required to achieve the goal. She should ensure that the goal realistically fits within the constraints of her time, energy, and financial means. For example, a person whose goal is to become a writer should ensure that she knows the requisites of good writing and is able to come up with a plan to consistently write and solicit the feedback needed to improve her craft.

Realistic: It is important to ascertain that a goal is conceivable and feasible and that it is consistent with other goals. A realistic goal is one that matters and is worth doing. This means that a person should condition her mindset to have a bias for action to attain the specified goal. For example, a person might set a realistic goal to lose weight but should know in advance that she will have to eat more healthfully and exercise consistently to achieve this goal. Similarly, while it is conceivable and feasible to have consistently happy relationships, no relationship is without its ups and downs. Women should be aware of this in advance and be willing to face disagreements and conflicts responsibly.

Time-Bound: A goal must have a target date by which it is expected to be achieved. Establishing a specific date creates a sense of urgency and determination for the task. Some goals can be achieved in short periods of time, while others may take years to accomplish. Establishing exact dates for achieving your goal will help you plan accordingly. For example, a person who wants to finish a college degree needs to estimate the amount of time required for school tasks. Based on the number of classes taken each semester and the requirements for each class, it becomes evident that he can finish his degree in four years.

Setting goals using the SMART framework ensures they are clear, actionable, and achievable, paving the way for personal and professional growth. By focusing on these elements, you can set effective goals that will lead you toward a more successful and fulfilling life.

CHAPTER 5

Question 4: How Do I Cultivate a Growth Mindset?

For many years, experts regarded intelligence as a fixed trait. However, Carol Dweck's 2006 book "Mindset: The New Psychology of Success" demonstrates that we have more control over our intelligence and abilities than previously believed. Her research showed that people fall into one of two categories when thinking about their abilities and intelligence: those with a growth mindset and those with a fixed mindset. Individuals with a growth mindset believe they can increase their intelligence and abilities through active learning, practice, and hard work. In contrast, those with a fixed mindset believe their intelligence and abilities are static and cannot significantly change. Dweck demonstrated that individuals with a growth mindset are more likely to succeed. With this knowledge, the following provides some guidance on how personal and professional development naturally occurs by leveraging a growth mindset.

Since the publication of Stanford University psychologist Carol Dweck's groundbreaking book "Mindset," the role of a growth mindset has become an emerging area of focus in personal and professional development. These ideas inject new energy into personal development because it is the individual's commitment to and actions based on a growth mindset that make long-term change possible. There is no overnight change, no quick fix, and no simple steps in this area of personal development. However, the good news is that when an individual works on developing a growth mindset, achieving consistent incremental change becomes a more positive and definite outcome.

The Power of a Growth Mindset

People often talk about having a "mindset" regarding their own and their team's potential, but what does it really mean? Essentially, there are two types of mindsets: one that sees potential through a lens of possibility (growth mindset) and another that views individual abilities as fixed and set in stone (fixed mindset).

The fixed mindset is a place where people are tethered to the belief that they can only accomplish things for which they have a natural talent. When someone with this mindset fails, they perceive the failure as catastrophic and unbearable, turning it into a crisis and, in some cases, a doorway to permanent disqualification.

Conversely, the growth mindset is a haven for lifelong learners. This mindset demonstrates open-mindedness to the possibility of acquiring talent in areas previously deemed unreachable. Moreover, individuals who harness the power of a growth mindset delight in the process of learning. Even when they falter or experience setbacks, they see these losses not as permanent demises but as opportunities to learn and improve continuously.

A fixed mindset can be appealing, especially in the early stages of an endeavor. When a person embarks on a new project and displays natural talent, there is an attraction to a sort of unwavering commitment that can make fixed-mindset thinking plausible. However, time and time again, as people share stories and lessons of their growth paths, we see that success is not achieved unless it is paired with an open-mindedness to fail, learn, and improve. Even the most naturally talented and skilled individuals were, at one point, beginners just like anyone else.

The pivotal difference between those who remain beginners and those who grow beyond their initial stages is the power of the growth mindset. Choosing to live from a place of growth-mindedness is one of the few decisions over which we have complete control. Embracing a growth mindset allows us to see challenges as opportunities, fosters resilience, and encourages continuous improvement.

In conclusion, cultivating a growth mindset involves a conscious effort to view intelligence and abilities as qualities that can be developed through dedication and hard work. It requires an openness to learning, a willingness to embrace challenges, and the resilience to persist in the face of setbacks. By adopting a growth mindset, you can unlock your potential for personal and professional growth, leading to a more fulfilling and successful life.

Ready to embrace the power of a growth mindset? Let's start the journey of continuous improvement together.

CHAPTER 6

Question 5: How Can I Improve My Time Management S

People will tolerate most failings in others better than they will poor time management. They know that when someone is consistently late or does not accomplish assigned tasks, it is disrespectful of their time and, by extension, of them. Why then do so many complain that they are ineffective at time management? When time management becomes an issue, it is usually a reflection of a deeper breakdown in the orderly progress of work, and hence in the work ethic. It is the subject of time management, though, rather than the more fundamental question of effective use of time, that excites widespread anxiety.

To begin to develop better time management skills, break your day into two-hour segments and, for one week, keep a log of all activities. Record how you use the segments. At the end of the week, review it and ask yourself how productively each day was spent and whether you felt in control of your life at all times. Initial reactions will likely be that you felt under pressure at certain times during the day's work, considered some activities a waste of time, and were amazed that an entire day could slip by with so little to show for it. The day was hijacked by others' requests, unsatisfactory work processes, computer network failures, and interruptions by colleagues. If all this sounds familiar, it is well to review time management principles.

Effective Time Management Strategies

To manage our time, we must manage ourselves. When we value ourselves, we choose how best to use our talents and abilities. When we allow ourselves no time for our thoughts, feelings, interests, and beliefs, we feel as if our time has been taken from us. In reality, it is we who give it away.

How do you currently manage the 168 hours available to you each week? Once you make the commitment to personal and professional development, here are some strategies for effective time management:

- **Get enough sleep to recharge your batteries:** Prioritize sleep to ensure you have the energy and focus needed for the day ahead.
- **Set aside a regular time for quiet reflection:** Use this time to think, plan, and assess your progress and goals.
- **Develop and follow a consistent daily schedule:** Routine helps in creating structure and discipline in your day.
- **Use a planner:** Track weekly, monthly, and yearly activities related to personal and professional development. A planner helps you stay organized and on top of your commitments.
- **Emphasize critical thinking classes and assignments:** These help improve your decision-making skills and efficiency.
- **Create a realistic to-do list:** Meet your daily, weekly, and monthly goals by listing tasks and prioritizing them.

- **Rate everything on your list:** A is essential, B is important, and C is desirable. Focus on the most critical activities first. Remember, "Hours of Hours" add up to a day.
- **Protect your work zone:** Find a consistent place where you can work without interruptions.
- **Set up a timetable for time-wasting activities:** Allocate specific times for phone or computer games, TV, and reading to ensure they don't interfere with productive tasks.
- **Make your precious commodity known:** No one can manage themselves effectively if others continually interrupt them. Consistently communicate your needs for time alone.

"Rising Higher: 12 Essential Questions for Personal and Professional Development" is a guidebook designed to help high school and college students develop a personal academic plan. It provides 12 essential personal and professional development questions to jumpstart your plan. By seriously answering these questions, students will consciously choose the courses, experiences, relationships, and jobs that will facilitate educational development, create lifelong learning patterns, and release the potential they hold inside. They will recognize their dreams and work to make them happen. This guidebook reduces overlap, gaps, and omissions in high school and college preparatory efforts. It provides a structured process to facilitate personal and career development at all stages of the learning process.

By adopting these time management strategies, you can take control of your day, reduce stress, and increase your productivity. Effective time management is a skill that will benefit you throughout your personal and professional life, helping you achieve your goals and reach your full potential. So, are you ready to take control of your time and make the most of every minute? Let's get started!

CHAPTER 7

Question 6: How Can I Enhance My Communication Ski

Effective communication can have a profound effect on every aspect of our lives. Our skill and style of communication, both in our personal and professional relationships, are determining factors in the quality of our interactions. The process of communication involves getting our ideas across and eliciting the intended reaction in our audience. Good communicators successfully manage these important exchanges. Whether it is a one-way or a two-way exchange, the ability to communicate successfully extends to listening and understanding, asking relevant questions, and being a clear, effective, responsive, and culturally sensitive speaker.

A key to behaving appropriately in any situation is to communicate openly, flexibly, and concisely. Understanding the situation, our relationship with others, and the goals we have in that situation helps us decide the role we need to play. We should prepare ourselves for various communication situations and respond in ways that are effective and appropriate to the needs of both our audience and ourselves. The objective of a successful communicator is to be understood the first time. Being an effective communicator ensures that the message is understood, encourages task completion, increases productivity, and strengthens relationships.

Key Communication Techniques

A manager's approach to situations and people can impact their work environment and ultimately their careers and personal goals. Here are some techniques to help enhance the way you interact with your staff and coworkers:

- **Words and Beyond:** The actual words you say amount to only a small portion of the message you send. It's not just what you say; it's how you say it, when you say it, where you say it, and to whom you say it. Nonverbal cues—such as facial expressions, gestures, and posture—facilitate communication and influence how others perceive and react to you. Your tone of voice and the language you use send equally powerful messages. We communicate using a combination of these verbal and nonverbal signals and behaviors.

- **Active Listening:** Effective communication is not just about speaking but also about listening. Active listening involves fully concentrating, understanding, responding, and remembering what is being said. It means engaging with the speaker, showing empathy, and providing feedback.

- **Open and Honest Communication:** Transparency in communication builds trust. Be open and honest about your thoughts and intentions. Encourage your team to do the same. When people feel trusted and valued, they are more likely to contribute positively.

- **Adaptability:** Flexibility in communication is crucial. Adapt your communication style to suit different situations and audiences. Be aware of cultural sensitivities and adjust your approach accordingly.

- **Clarity and Conciseness:** Be clear and concise in your communication. Avoid jargon and be straightforward to ensure that your message is easily understood. This minimizes the risk of misinterpretation.
- **Nonverbal Communication:** Pay attention to your body language, facial expressions, and gestures. Nonverbal communication can reinforce or contradict what you are saying. Be mindful of these cues to ensure your message is consistent.
- **Feedback and Follow-Up:** Provide constructive feedback and encourage feedback from others. Follow up on conversations to ensure that tasks are completed and any issues are addressed.

Indeed, much of the work of a manager is communication. Many of the management problems we confront—such as power struggles, resistance to change, personal chemistry difficulties, and fear of confrontation—reflect interpersonal dynamics. Consequently, you need to build an environment of trust. Your willingness to encourage a spirit of respect and civility and to practice good communication will inspire your team to do the same.

You may have to change some of your management methods, but over the long term, your team will become more effective and "user friendly." Building respect and civil treatment requires effort, but your success as a team leader depends on it. A good leader can not only make things better for the staff but also improve the delivery of care to clients. Set an example by practicing the skills you'd like your team members to adopt.

Enhancing your communication skills is an ongoing process that involves self-awareness, practice, and a willingness to learn and adapt. By focusing on these key techniques, you can become a more effective communicator, improve your relationships, and achieve your personal and professional goals. Ready to take your communication skills to the next level? Let's get started!

Question 7: What Is the Importance of Building Res

While climbing the mountain of life, failure is inevitable. How can we build resilience within ourselves to prepare for adversity and trials along our path? If life is going to be a tightrope, how can we build courage and resources to stay balanced and not fear the inevitable slip? Is there a simple test to see what kind of resources you have to meet adversity? How much growth are you willing to endure? When life gives you lemons, can you make lemonade and even profit from selling it to children or other passersby?

Helping and encouraging others, as well as reaching out when you need help, is crucial. Caring, polite, and helpful behavior influences your own feelings and helps you build a supportive network. Giving back to others also strengthens this network.

Get enough sleep. People who are critically sleep-deprived report lower performance and higher stress levels in interactions, including those with others. Propel yourself to sleep well by building an optimal recovery environment. For example, darken the bedroom, reduce noise, create a mental wind-down routine before retiring, and avoid drinking a large amount of liquid approximately two hours before sleeping.

Sometimes, staying angry can be productive, especially for women. Expressing what one is angry about can actually be productive, with benefits for goal achievement. Moreover, expressed anger can have important psychological and physical benefits. In certain circumstances, anger can provide additional motivation to seek support from your network and further motivation to fight or work harder as needed.

Developing Resilience in the Face of Challenges

The need to become more resilient has become an essential part of our current work environment. People encounter unexpected shocks and unwanted news almost daily, often leading to several difficult hurdles that need to be overcome. Learning to deal with these issues and their consequences is crucial to our overall success. Seeking to understand an individual's relationship with resilience is an essential component of developing resilience. Questions that reveal how this critical attribute works can be invaluable for client development, coaching, consulting, or other valuable individual discussion opportunities. These questions are engaging enough to elicit self-reflection and the sharing of important thoughts and feelings.

A few questions can help individuals understand the meaning and significance of resilience in their lives and delve into potential personal development that could elevate their personal and professional selves. For people of all ages and experiences, resilience is a powerful attribute that denotes internal fortitude, courage, and confidence in one's abilities. By recognizing a person's current resilience and development, you offer them the opportunity to grow and learn from difficult life issues. This can lead to greater self-awareness, understanding, and insight. Such important matters are vital for those who wish to be effective leaders, those already in leadership positions, those who wish to work as partners among groups of workers, and those who lead significant personal and professional lives.

In conclusion, building resilience is about preparing ourselves for the inevitable challenges of life. It's about developing a support network, maintaining our physical and mental health, and leveraging our emotions, like anger, for positive outcomes. By focusing on these aspects, we can enhance our resilience, enabling us to handle adversity with courage and grace.

Ready to build some resilience and take on the world? Let's get started on this journey together!

CHAPTER 9

Question 8: How Can I Foster Creativity and Innova

We only have to think of the surrealists, who had great disdain for any form of communication directed to appeasing the public. The problem was not that they did not know what people were thinking and needing, it was that, for them, these were not interesting. They saw the truly interesting and positive restlessness of people as a malleable material for experimentation. Thus, the question is, how can we put our current potential—the restless and curious nature of people—to innovative use?

Traditionally, work has been the domain of business, while innovation has resided in research institutes and laboratories. However, scientific and creative activity is breaking out of these usual confines. Researchers and innovators are found in all types of professions, even among business leaders, as well as people envisioning new disciplines and professions. So, what is creativity really? Is it the dawn, breaking into the world with the light of a new scientific discovery or philosophical school of thought? Or is it the night, creeping forward in the dark, as we sense future market needs and develop products that have yet to be invented?

If creativity is special, extraordinary, and generative—giving not only direction but also conceptual elements—how can we stimulate it? Is it effective to encourage creators to pursue their boundless passions and talents, regardless of where they lead? Or is it better to expose them to multiple problems and deliberately restrict certain fields of action? Should we encourage every creator to explore within their domains or to look beyond them? How can we choose the best way to stimulate creativity?

Finally, how do we motivate creators? If creativity is future-directed towards collective advantage, finding satisfaction in knowing that its core aims to define and share common objectives, why then are gifts used to certify absolute uniqueness? In other words, if an artist or intellectual's motivation is to be part of the collective, why is this very collective always pushing them towards absolute individuality, segregating them from the collective?

Encouraging Creativity in Problem-Solving

Some revenue professionals have not yet learned that there is more than one way to solve a particular problem and still succeed. There is often substantial benefit in solving problems with a view toward encouraging further creativity, rather than simply correcting what is usually assumed to be one "mistake." One need only look at the ever-decreasing number of world-class corporations that once dominated their industries, such as A&P, Westinghouse, Pan-Am, and others, to see the value of creativity in problem-solving.

To the question "How will creativity be encouraged in the solution?" we might add: "Before we feel we've 'solved' the problem by replacing an entirely different part, could we search briefly for other components with the same specifications, maybe costing one-tenth as much and made from material less prone to fatigue or wear?" Not all corporations automatically discourage the free and enthusiastic voice of innovators. In fact, a very simple revenue forecasting solution, an equationological formula for a straight line, was given the nickname "Charlie's Fudge-and-Hunch Forecast" by my grateful operational colleague. In one of his earliest days working in this country, after rapidly surveying the figures, Charlie provided the only forecast accounting had received in the demand-modification effort he had just begun. It was quick to prepare and obviously overdue. Afterward, production was excited by his production-planning colleague's next demand report showing a sudden, unexpected drop. However, production was disappointed the next day when a second Charlie forecast took exactly as long to prepare and showed no shortfalls, reducing the excitement felt the day before.

In conclusion, fostering creativity and innovation involves understanding the restless and curious nature of people, encouraging them to explore and experiment, and motivating them by recognizing their contributions and supporting their unique talents. By embracing different perspectives and creative problem-solving approaches, we can drive innovation and achieve remarkable results. Ready to unleash your creative potential? Let's get started on fostering a culture of innovation!

CHAPTER 10

Question 9: How Can I Develop Leadership Skills?

In addition to personal frameworks of understanding that have prepared you to serve in a particular industry of choice, it is wise to develop leadership skills alongside or in conjunction with your more traditional educational plans. In almost every personal and public sector, individuals capable of taking on a leadership role possess wisdom and a varied skill set that enables them to master enigmas, heartily accept challenges, adapt to the nature of leadership, and regulate themselves, their organizations, and their constituents.

While you are acquiring new knowledge to ensure the economic viability of you and your family, do not underestimate the need for good leadership skills. The ability to provide emotional appeal, set sound goals, define missions, assign roles, and secure results are essential leadership assets in any human endeavor. Becoming a leader is not easy, nor is assuming a role where brave decisions must be made. The best leaders are simple in their approach, allowing their mission and organization to speak louder than they do. Leaders serve their organization and require the satisfaction of their constituents to keep the team together.

Small organizations usually demand good emotional appeal and adherence to certain customs, while larger organizations tend to lean more toward strategic planning, interpersonal skills, and dependable delivery. In organizations with many layers of management, leaders need to sense unrest and keep morale alive. They must also create an atmosphere of discipline.

Essential Components of Effective Leadership

Effective leadership is the extent to which a leader can influence creativity and innovation, guide strategic change, and nurture a culture in which employees have the courage to embrace bold thinking. However, effective leadership also includes pragmatism and focuses on the consideration of the implications of an idea under consideration. Here, we will consider three essential components of effective leadership: strategic perspective, influencing capabilities, and realizing the full potential of team members. Together, these components range from the strategic, overall direction of the organization to the capacity to embrace and implement bold ideas to achieve success, to nurturing the environment in which these strategic imperatives can be realized.

Strategic Perspective: This capability focuses on the long-term implications of decisions and activities, and the probable causes and effects. It involves assessing various strategies that may be utilized to attain the organization's vision. A clear and compelling vision of the organization's future is essential, as is expertise in perseverance and overcoming obstacles.

Influencing Capabilities: Communication is key, as is the ability to interact with a wide spectrum of stakeholders. Leaders need to create a climate of steady, visible leadership, especially in the aftermath of major challenges, and unify individuals around common goals. Building trust and support internally and externally, and pooling knowledge and resources within and outside the organization—including cross-functional resources—is crucial. A leader must demonstrate resilience following rejection or adversity.

Realizing the Full Potential of Team Members: Effective leaders understand the strengths and weaknesses of their team members and work to develop their potential. They provide opportunities for growth, offer constructive feedback, and encourage innovation and creativity. By nurturing their team, leaders can foster a supportive environment that drives success.

Developing leadership skills involves continuous learning, self-awareness, and a commitment to personal and professional growth. By focusing on these essential components, you can enhance your leadership capabilities and make a meaningful impact on your organization and the people you lead.

Ready to develop your leadership skills and take on new challenges? Let's embark on this journey together and unleash your full potential as a leader.

CHAPTER 11

Question 10: What Is the Role of Emotional Intelli

Everyone is talking about emotional intelligence (EI or EQ) these days. Are they over-hyping its importance, or is it truly integral to our success and individual happiness? Empirical data supports the latter; EI can be as important as intelligence quotient (IQ) in predicting life success, including relationship success. While EQ influences a wide variety of individual relationships, its significance in group relations—how teams and societies work—is less clear. So what actually is EI? It is the awareness, understanding, and ability to control emotions in oneself and in others. The emotional intelligence model has four aspects:

Self- and Social-Awareness: Do you recognize your emotions when they occur? Are you aware as you are feeling and less likely to be overwhelmed by them? Do you understand why you feel that way? While the capacity to be aware of emotions is predominantly a personal trait, social-awareness (empathy) results from a combination of understanding those emotions and acting accordingly. Satisfaction in both personal and professional spheres depends, at least partly, on these qualities.

Understanding Emotional Intelligence

Emotional intelligence (EQ) refers to a person's ability to recognize and understand emotions in themselves and others. This includes the capability to manage one's own emotions while considering the emotions of others. People with a high level of EQ can use their skills to work with others more effectively, which is why emotional intelligence has become a buzzword in management.

One study found that plumbers who earned their living based on how well they interacted with customers generally made more money than their less emotionally intelligent colleagues. Growing research has shown a strong positive relationship between high EQ and professional as well as personal success. Conversely, low EQ might explain why some professionals who are technically skilled may fail to be promoted or serve as effective leaders. EQ has also been shown to have a negative impact on career success for people who are easily stressed, anxious, and readily upset. These individuals may struggle to recognize and manage their emotions, potentially increasing job stress for everyone around them.

In this section, you will be introduced to a more detailed model of emotional intelligence that has been proven to translate directly to better human performance. Goleman's model of EQ has been validated and shown to be closely associated with several other concepts such as motivation and social skills. You will be guided to the many sources of emotional intelligence, find some exercises to start improving, and explore some of the many applications of EQ.

EQ in Personal and Professional Success: The significance of emotional intelligence in personal and professional settings cannot be overstated. In personal relationships, high EQ individuals tend to have more meaningful and satisfying interactions. They can navigate conflicts, understand their partner's perspective, and foster deeper connections. Professionally, EQ is critical for effective leadership, teamwork, and customer relations. Leaders with high EQ can inspire and motivate their teams, manage stress, and create a positive work environment.

Components of Emotional Intelligence:

1. **Self-Awareness:** The ability to recognize and understand your emotions as they happen. This includes being aware of the effect of your emotions on others. Self-awareness allows you to stay in control and make better decisions.
2. **Self-Regulation:** The ability to manage your emotions and impulses. Self-regulation involves self-discipline, reliability, and adaptability. It helps you respond to situations calmly and constructively.
3. **Motivation:** A passion for work that goes beyond money and status. High EQ individuals are motivated by a deeply embedded desire to achieve for the sake of achievement.
4. **Empathy:** The ability to understand the emotions of others. Empathy involves recognizing others' emotional states and responding appropriately. It is essential for building strong relationships and managing social interactions effectively.
5. **Social Skills:** Proficiency in managing relationships and building networks. Social skills include effective communication, conflict resolution, and cooperation.

Improving Emotional Intelligence:

- **Practice Self-Awareness:** Keep a journal to track your emotions and the situations that trigger them. Reflect on how your emotions influence your actions.
- **Develop Self-Regulation:** Practice techniques such as mindfulness, deep breathing, and meditation to manage stress and stay calm under pressure.

- **Enhance Motivation:** Set personal goals that align with your values and interests. Celebrate small achievements along the way to stay motivated.
- **Cultivate Empathy:** Practice active listening. Pay attention to body language and verbal cues to better understand others' emotions.
- **Build Social Skills:** Engage in social activities, join groups, and volunteer to enhance your interpersonal skills.

In conclusion, emotional intelligence is a critical factor in achieving personal and professional success. By understanding and managing your emotions and developing empathy and social skills, you can improve your interactions, build stronger relationships, and achieve your goals. Are you ready to enhance your EQ and unlock your full potential? Let's get started on this journey!

CHAPTER 12

Question 11: How Can I Build and Maintain Healthy

Success and well-being are all about relationships. The ability to build constructive and empathic relationships is a skill that can be developed. Despite the changes in contemporary society, the need for true connections has not diminished. Anthropologists of any time period will tell us, "True connections are what make us human." As Brene Brown aptly puts it, "Connections are what give purpose and meaning to our lives."

When was the last time someone genuinely asked, "Would you like to refresh our connection and discuss this?" It's not about the quantity of time but the quality of time and contact. A bright sparkle of happiness and delight in the person's eyes is a sure sign of a well-connected relationship. What about relationships? Are they all that important? If the relationship is toxic, maybe not. But a generally independent person who claims they don't need anyone else in their lives is not speaking the truth.

First, we need to acknowledge that we build many casual relationships, and these are as important as the most stable and deep ones.

The Foundations of Healthy Relationships

Good projects always start with strong foundations. Wonderful, high-rise, glittering ideas can easily turn into sudden and dramatic failures without these great bases. This first module of our text is about personal and professional development and is supported by what can be considered the most solid base for high-rise achievements: healthy relationships. Take it as a piece of helpful advice.

You might be new to the professional world or even a top-level businessman. Somehow, you must be part of it, and it has the potential to affect you and be affected by you. The same can be said about your personal life. As this set of chapters is mainly dedicated to facilitating personal and professional development, relationships are the focus, not the main themes. Being so important to life, trying to emphasize or rank the importance of relationships is not the intention here. I would rather state the obvious – for going higher and higher, you must first secure strong and safe foundations.

Understanding the Importance of Relationships: Relationships are the bedrock of personal and professional success. They provide support, collaboration, and the exchange of ideas, making it possible to achieve goals that would be difficult alone.

Building Relationships: To build strong relationships, start by being open and authentic. People are drawn to those who are genuine and transparent. Show interest in others by asking questions and actively listening to their responses. Find common ground and shared interests to foster a sense of connection.

Maintaining Relationships: Maintaining healthy relationships requires ongoing effort. Regularly communicate and check in with people, whether through calls, messages, or face-to-face meetings. Show appreciation and gratitude, and be willing to offer help and support when needed.

Navigating Conflict: Conflicts are inevitable in any relationship. The key is to handle them constructively. Address issues directly but respectfully, and aim for a resolution that satisfies both parties. Practice empathy by understanding the other person's perspective and finding common ground.

Balancing Casual and Deep Relationships: Both casual and deep relationships are important. Casual relationships can provide a wide network of support and opportunities, while deep relationships offer emotional support and a sense of belonging. Nurture both types to create a well-rounded support system.

Creating Quality Time: Quality time is more important than the quantity of time spent with someone. Engage in meaningful activities, have in-depth conversations, and create shared experiences that strengthen your bond.

Recognizing Toxic Relationships: Not all relationships are beneficial. It's important to recognize toxic relationships that drain your energy and negatively impact your well-being. Set boundaries and, if necessary, distance yourself from such relationships to maintain your mental and emotional health.

By focusing on these foundational aspects, you can build and maintain healthy relationships that contribute to your overall success and happiness. So, are you ready to strengthen your connections and enrich your life through healthy relationships? Let's embark on this journey together!

Question 12: How Can I Achieve Work-Life Balance?

The work-life balance question is a critical one: **How can I achieve work-life balance?** This overarching question requires us to step back and look at our lives, wants, needs, and dreams from a broader perspective. Work-life balance isn't just about transitions. It encompasses various aspects of your life, akin to the Finish Line Question. It includes your families, friends, and communities, allowing you to contemplate the kind of legacy you want to leave. It is as personal as your reflections about Question 11 and can be considered in the same ways, both individually and collectively.

Is your personal balance sheet in life holding steady or showing a deficit? We all have limited resources and need to think carefully before spending them recklessly. While some organizations may not need additional chairpersons, consider helping with Student Ambassadors or sponsoring a work-study student. Nonprofit organizations are always looking for good board members and committees. Even short-term service opportunities can lead to long-term rewards.

Money is not the most important thing in life; yet, to paraphrase one of the most overused quotes of all time, without some, we are nothing but a bag of bones! Society places a high priority on those with financial and societal success. From a practical perspective, in our culture, money certainly impacts our ability to enjoy life. Our job is both the easiest and the most difficult place to make changes to achieve our personal goals. Small changes add up over time. A lot of people mock the idea of work-life balance, but let them. Relax. If work-life balance is less important in their definition of success, then they have achieved that balance in their lives—something much harder than it sounds! Value the importance of stepping back to ensure that the list you are counting truly reflects your life and pursuits. Small shifts now can put your life on steadier ground. Making bigger changes may be necessary to steer you back on course.

Strategies for Balancing Work and Personal Life

Recognizing the importance of work-life balance as a primary goal and continually working toward it is crucial. Both personal and general suggestions are offered below, with the hope that these can form the basis for developing new and personal strategies to meet individual needs in both personal growth and professional development.

1. Be a Support System: Create an environment that encourages individuality while sharing yourself with others. Encourage your family or friends to share their time and interests with you and be supportive.

2. Time for Education: Consider career development by going back to school. Continuous learning can enhance your skills and open new opportunities.

3. Establish Daily Needs: Devote some time each day to your interests and passions. This helps in maintaining a sense of fulfillment and balance.

4. Don't Let Anyone Judge: Accept yourself and grant yourself permission to be who you are and strive to be who you wish to be. Self-acceptance is crucial for personal well-being.

5. Prioritize Health: Ensure you get adequate sleep, exercise regularly, and maintain a healthy diet. Physical well-being is foundational to achieving balance.

6. Set Boundaries: Clearly define your work and personal time. Communicate these boundaries to your colleagues and family to manage expectations.

7. Use Technology Wisely: Leverage technology to streamline tasks but be mindful of its overuse. Unplugging occasionally is essential for mental health.

8. Delegate Tasks: Don't hesitate to delegate tasks at work and home. Sharing responsibilities can lighten your load and reduce stress.

9. Pursue Hobbies: Engage in activities that you enjoy and that help you unwind. Hobbies can be a great way to relax and rejuvenate.

10. Reflect and Adjust: Regularly assess your work-life balance and make adjustments as needed. Life is dynamic, and your balance may require periodic reevaluation.

Maintaining a sense of balance in work and personal life is essential for self-esteem and an integral aspect of personal development. By adopting these strategies, you can create a harmonious balance that fosters both personal and professional growth. Are you ready to achieve a work-life balance that enriches your life and pursuits? Let's embark on this journey together!

CHAPTER 14

Conclusion: Reflecting on Your Personal and Profes

The theme of this book is "Rising Higher: 12 Essential Questions for Personal and Professional Development." This theme relates to the factors one often encounters at various junctures in life, particularly during college, early professional development years, and critical career advancement stages. It is worth it—and often most meaningful—to pause and reflect from time to time, engaging in "Reflecting on Your Personal and Professional Development Journey."

For many of you, it may also be a time to return home and further realize the importance and grounding influence of your family and hometown. Otherwise, you may have blazed onto the fast track, not having had serious time to stop, think, reflect, or evaluate.

To refresh your recollection, in Chapter 1, the early part focused on "How To Be Wise: Problems and Questioning." The use of questioning is a technique directly applicable to the key elements of the motivational process and wisdom. As you facilitate others in learning, continue to use questioning to expose yourself to areas you need to learn to be better prepared to adapt. By asking more of the questions that get at the essential nature of the problem, both you and your protégés will rise to higher levels of understanding and ability to relate and contribute to the overall knowledge of the process.

Moreover, in the analogy of sports coaching, an exceptional coach not only knows the game but also has the instinctive ability to distill pertinent technical aspects and communicate them in easily understood terms.

Reflecting on your journey allows you to assess your growth, understand your motivations, and realign your goals with your evolving values and aspirations. It is a time to celebrate your achievements, learn from your experiences, and plan for future endeavors. Here are some steps to guide your reflection process:

1. **Review Your Goals:** Revisit the goals you set at different stages of your journey. Evaluate how well you've met these goals and the challenges you encountered.
2. **Assess Your Growth:** Reflect on your personal and professional growth. Consider the skills you've developed, the knowledge you've gained, and the experiences that have shaped you.
3. **Recognize Milestones:** Identify and celebrate the milestones and achievements along your journey. Acknowledging these successes boosts your confidence and motivation.
4. **Analyze Challenges:** Reflect on the obstacles and setbacks you've faced. Analyze how you dealt with them, what you learned, and how they contributed to your development.
5. **Set New Goals:** Based on your reflection, set new goals that align with your current values and aspirations. Make these goals specific, measurable, achievable, relevant, and time-bound (SMART).

6. **Seek Feedback:** Engage with mentors, peers, and colleagues to gain insights and feedback on your journey. Their perspectives can provide valuable guidance and encouragement.

7. **Plan for the Future:** Create a plan for your next steps, incorporating the lessons learned and the goals set during your reflection. Ensure this plan is flexible and adaptable to changing circumstances.

Reflecting on your personal and professional development journey is an ongoing process that requires time, honesty, and a willingness to grow. By taking the time to reflect, you can gain a deeper understanding of yourself, your motivations, and your goals, ultimately leading to a more fulfilling and successful life.

So, are you ready to rise higher and continue your journey of personal and professional development? Let's embark on this path together, armed with insights and a renewed sense of purpose.